I0108811

THE

VISITOR'S GUIDE

TO

BOURNEMOUTH,

AND ITS NEIGHBOURHOOD;

INCLUDING NOTICES OF THE

CHIEF OBJECTS OF INTEREST

WITHIN A DISTANCE OF NINE MILES.

THIRD EDITION.

LONDON.

ACKERMAN, 96, STRAND.

SYDENHAM, BOURNEMOUTH AND POOLE.

1850.

CONTENTS.

CONTENTS.

BOURNEMOUTH

AND ITS ENVIRONS.

THE traveller on the western coast of Hampshire, when approaching the confines of that county and its junction with Dorsetshire, passes over a tract of dark heath land, scarcely diversified by the thick and sombre fir plantations that have sprung up in various parts, during the last few years, and which give to the neighbourhood a peculiar and not uninteresting character. Midway between Christchurch and Poole, the road conducts the traveller into a narrow vale winding into the land and opening directly upon the sea shore, and on entering which he is delighted with the prospect of social life, animated retirement, and a combination of the elegancies of nature and of art, spread before his view; detached villas, indicating every variety of style that the fancy and ingenuity of the architect could devise, and admirably associating with the local natural features, rows of stately edifices, relieved by the dark foliage of dense plantations, extensive walks, and tastefully arranged shrubberies, are the objects that first strike the eye in this pleasing retreat; whilst the whole is softened by an air of tranquil repose and a quietude of character eminently grateful to those who seek a relaxation from the fatigue and excitement of fashionable life, or a respite from the turmoils and anxieties of rough intercourse with the world.

This pleasing spot,

"Embowered in trees and hardly known to fame,"

the beauties of which are enhanced by the contrast afforded by the surrounding scenery, is Bournemouth, where, in a brief season, the magic hand of enterprise converted the silent and unfrequented vale into the gay resort of fashion and the favoured retreat of the invalid.

Bournemouth, which is situated at the south-west extremity of the county of Hants, is so named as being the embouchure of the " Bourne" (which word is the Anglo-Saxon generic term for " rivulet"), a stream rising about six miles off, in the adjoining parish of Kinson, and which, after running through the intervening valley, here finds its way into the sea through one of those chines that give so pleasing a character to this part of the coast. It is locally comprised in the tything of Holdenhurst, and in the borough of Christchurch, is five miles from that town and five from the neighbouring port of Poole.

A decoy pond was formerly established here for the capture of wild fowl, which frequent the neighbourhood in great numbers during the winter season, for which purpose the quiet and secluded character of the locality was eminently adapted. From this circumstance the place was generally known by the abbreviated name of the 'Coypond.

It is now nearly forty years since the scenery and capabilities of this retreat were first appreciated by L. D. G. Tregonwell, Esq., of Cranborne, Dorset, who possessed a considerable portion of the then barren heath land which existed every where in the immediate neighbourhood. Delighted with the sheltered situation, the genial temperature that prevailed here at all seasons, the magnificent seaward prospect, and the tranquil retirement that might here be successfully sought, he erected a mansion which became his favourite residence, and surrounded it with shrubberies and plantations, this within the last few years has been called Exeter House, in compliment to the Marquis of Exeter, by whom it has, on more than one occasion, been occupied. Mr. Tregonwell also built an inn by the side of the road, then but little frequented, and a few cottages, which were occasionally resorted to in the bathing season by invalids desirous of availing themselves of the advantages offered by the natural peculiarities of the spot.

In the plantation, about two minutes walk from the mansion, was erected a cenotaph to the memory

of Mr. Tregonwell,* who after the erection of his
mansion spent a great portion of his time here
but died at the family seat at Cranborne, Dorset,
in 1832, and was buried in the neighbouring
parish of Anderson. His remains, however, together
with those of an infant son, were removed thence and
deposited in a vault in the churchyard of this place
on the 20th of January, 1846. His widow, who was
equally attached to Bournemouth, survived him till
April, 1846, when she died at Bournemouth, and was
buried in the same vault.

It was reserved however, for Sir G. W. Tapps
Gervis, Bart., of Hinton Admiral, near Christchurch,
to give an efficient impetus to the improvements of
which the place was capable. About 14 years since,
being the principal landowner of the neighbourhood,
he became satisfied that Bournemouth was endowed
by nature with those especial features and circum-
stances which eminently fitted it to become an approv-
ed resort of those, who, at the termination of the
London season, seek on the coast that invigorating

---

* The Cenotaph, a massive Pedestal surmounted by an Urn, bears the
following Inscription :—
" This Urn
Marks the favourite Spot of
L. D. G. Tregonwell,
late of Cranborne Lodge, Dorset, Esq.
The first Proprietor resident
at Bournemouth,
And to his beloved memory
is dedicated,
By his Widow Henrietta,
Daughter of Henry William Portman, Esq.,
1832."

repose, and that commixture of fashion and retirement which afford the best protection against ennui, and are most conducive to the restoration of that freshness and activity, both in the physical and mental functions, which the constant excitements of town life have so great a tendency to undermine. Under his auspices therefore, and directed by the acknowledged talent and personal superintendence of Mr. B. Ferry, the eminent architect, many plans for the improvement of the estate were laid down and some of them immediately realized. Thus on spots where before the foot of man rarely pressed, but the lowly heath flower blossomed and faded in unnoticed solitude—where no sound was heard but the rustling of the rank grass and the wild shrub as they waved in the light sea breeze,—there a number of detached villas, each marked by distinct and peculiar architectural features, have sprung into existence, affording accommodation of varying extent, so as to be suited to the convenience of either large or small families, and adapted, some for extended, others for confined, establishments. To all these are attached ample gardens, whilst in the front of the principal row, called from its having a westerly aspect " Westover Villas," are shrubberies tastefully laid out and walks arranged with due regard to convenience and effect. At one end of this range of Westover Villas, stands a spacious and commodious hotel, erected for the accommodation of more temporary visitants, and fitted up in the most complete style. All these edifices command views of the ocean, of the distant coast, and of the vale lying immediately beneath, whilst the site is, at the same time, so judiciously chosen that they are effectually sheltered from the biting winds of the north and east.

Still more recently, a transfer of the extensive Bruce property, ranging from this vale far to the westward, has been followed by further and still progressive improvements.   A range of stately houses, now designated as "Richmond Terrace," in which a dignified exterior is combined with the most complete internal accommodation, has been erected, environed by plantations which it is proposed should be intersected by walks and drives of considerable length and imposing character. A number of Villas of a less pretending class, and calculated for the accommodation of persons with small families, or of limited means, have been erected on the Tregonwell property facing the road leading to Poole, and which, in consequence of the shops being situated in that quarter, is known as "Commercial Road."

VIEWS.

The marine prospect presented from the summit of the sandy cliffs that overhang the beach is alike pleasing and extensive, and, whilst the ocean waves break slowly on the shore, where the

> ———— "murmuring tone
> Of waters mellowed into music dies,
> Like that which echoes from the world afar,
> Or lingers round the path of perished years,"

the eye glances over the wide expanse included in a bay that extends from Hengistbury head, off Christchurch, on the east, to Durlestone head, beyond Swanage on the west; the more prominent objects of interest being the picturesque cliffs of the Isle of Wight, with Saint Catherine's head, Alum Bay, the Needle Rocks, and the towering earthwork of Hengistbury head eastward; and westward are the town of Swanage, nestled under the dark outline of Durlestone promontory, the Purbeck hills, with the isolated pinnacles familiarly known by the forbidding appellation of Old Harry, the adjacent sylvan scenery surrounding the secluded village of Studland, and the majestic ruins of Corfe Castle.

The full sweep of the English Channel which is here commanded often presents a most animated appearance, especially when a change of wind is followed by the passing of a great number of vessels of all descriptions respectively up or down the channel; and the nearer approach of the craft running between the Isle of Wight and the mainland offers an additional feature of interest to this locality.

THE BEACH.

The Beach, easy of access, forms a delightful promenade at any state of the tide, being of a fine firm sand; and a walk under the cliffs, either to the east or west, in addition to the usual charms of a marine prospect, will be amply repaid by the striking scenery presented by the several chines that are to be found running inland, and which form so peculiar and pleasing a feature of the tertiary formation.

BATHING.

The healthful recreation of open sea bathing may be enjoyed here at any hour; the machines, which are well attended, being very convenient, and always available.

A suite of commodious warm baths, combining every desirable accessory, has been erected immediately contiguous to the beach, and the managers, Mr. and Mrs. Pratt, are at all times most attentive.

MARKETS AND COMMUNICATIONS.

Bournemouth is well supplied with provisions and necessaries of all kinds, several shops having been opened; and the place being within an easy reach of the plentifully supplied, and cheap markets of Poole, no difficulty whatever is experienced. The opportunities of intercourse with other parts of the kingdom are numerous and convenient, there being six omnibuses daily between this and the town of Poole, and two daily from and to Christchurch, all in communication with the South-Western Railway. From Christchurch is a coach daily to and from Salisbury. From the Dorchester terminus of the South-Western Railway, coaches run to Weymouth, Bridport, and many other places to

Weymouth, Bridport, and many other places to the westward, as well as to Sherborne, Yeovil, and other towns in that direction. Facilities for visiting the Isle of Wight and the south-east coast may be found at Lymington and Southampton.

The islands of Guernsey and Jersey, and the Continent, are easily accessible from Southampton. Steam communication is also about to be established between Poole and the Channel Islands.

POST.

A daily Post is established between Bourne-mouth and Poole, arriving at the former place at nine A.M., and departing thence at a quarter past six o'clock, P.M. The Post Office is conveniently situate near the Tregonwell's Arms Inn, in the centre of the place.

THE CHURCH.

The church is a very neat, though small, structure, consisting of nave and chancel, free from any super-fluous ornament, and having a very elegant painted window at the east end. It affords accommodation for 350 persons and was erected in the year 1844, on a commodious site, at the sole expense of Sir G. W. Tapps Gervis, Bart., the owner of the soil. It stands in a large church yard, the portion of which that has already been appropriated to purposes of sepulture being laid out with much taste, and kept in excellent order. Divine Service commences on

Sundays at 11 o'clock in the forenoon, and at 4 in the afternoon, except during a portion of the winter when the afternoon service commences at three o'clock. There is also a service commencing at eight o'clock daily throughout the year. The incumbent is the Rev. A. M. Bennett.

The National and Sunday Schools in connection with the Church are well patronized, and the Rev. Mr. Bennett proves a most energetic patron leaving no stone unturned to render them what he conceives such schools ought to be. The children until very recently assembled in a building, which, prior to the erection of the present church, was used for the purpose of divine worship, but the result of the rapid increase of Bournemouth, and the perseverance of the incumbent of the church is, that this building being found not sufficiently capacious for the requirements of the school, a subscription was raised for the purpose, and commodious and very substantial school buildings have just been erected, the foundation stone of which was laid on the 29th of June, this year.

THE PARSONAGE HOUSE.

A large and substantial building, on an eminence, surrounded by pleasure gardens, and commanding most extensive views, is the Parsonage House, erected by the present incumbent in 1846, from designs by Mr. Pearce, Architect of Canford, who also furnished the design for the school buildings above alluded to.

INDEPENDENT CHAPEL.

In the summer of 1849, a plain building of some capacity was erected in the western part of Bournemouth, and opened as a meeting house for a congregation of Independent dissenters.

THE HOTELS.

The "Bath Hotel" is a very elegant, spacious, and convenient structure, capable of affording accommodation to a great number of inmates. The regulations and arrangements, under the attentive superintendence and careful management of the occupier, Miss Toomer, are such as to ensure the comfort and tend to the satisfaction of the visitors. The situation of this hotel is eminently delightful; the many beautiful sitting and other rooms are admirably arranged; and the views from its different aspects are varied, extensive, and pleasing, commanding on the one front a magnificent seaward prospect, with the distant coast of the Isle of Purbeck, and, on the other the full sweep of the valley of the Bourne. The spacious grounds attached to the house have been laid out with much taste, in gardens, shrubberies, and plantations.

The "Belle Vue Hotel" is a commodious building, situate close to the beach, and affording excellent accommodation. It is at present under the management of Mr. ^XMateham, from the Royal Hotel, Southampton, and like the Bath Hotel, has pleasure gardens attached.

THE LIBRARY.

Amongst the essentials of a watering-place, a Library and News Room, affording that mental recreation the enjoyment of which is indispensable to true comfort, ranks highly, and such an institution has accordingly been founded. Being most delightfully situated in immediate proximity to the beach, which it fronts, and commanding a beautiful marine prospect, it forms a choice promenade for the lounger, whilst a plentiful supply of books, magazines, and newspapers, proffers information as to the course of the busy world, and presents sources of intellectual amusement and intelligence.

MEDICAL ADVANTAGES.

The invalid will here find a Physician and Surgeon, both of considerable skill and experience ; and also a Chemist, supplying articles of the very first quality.

NATURAL HISTORY.

It does not accord with the purpose of the present work to enter into those scientific details which may well become the pages of a larger and more pretending work, but it is desirable to direct attention to the leading outlines of this portion of the subject.

Climate, &c.—The climate of the south coast of England generally, has long been established by professional preference, as eminently adapted for the restoration of the invalid and the preservation of health, from the prevalence of a mild and genial atmosphere, presenting a combination in due proportions of the essential properties of heat, dryness and humidity. And, whilst such is the general character of this line of coast, it is proved by medical experience, meteorological observations, and botanical indications, that the qualities which are involved in the formation of this character, are especially to be found at Bournemouth, this pre-eminence arising from its situation and local peculiarities. Placed at the mouth of a pleasant valley, and surrounded by gentle hills on all sides but the south, to which it opens to the sea, Bournemouth is particularly warm, the heat, however, being refreshingly tempered by the soft sea breeze; and the temperature is, moreover, equable in a surprising degree, the variations of the thermometer being far less than occur in most other places.

Geological Features.—The district in which Bournemouth is situated, is a portion of that branch of the tertiary formation denominated the Isle of Wight Basin. The prevailing feature of this district, extending from Poole harbour to Hengistbury head, consists of undulating hills of white, yellow, and grey sands, interspersed with beds of plastic clay; and apparently there is not a particle of calcareous matter. The cliffs which constitute the coast, vary in height from 50 to upwards of 150 feet. They present vast masses of sand, with the clay beds occurring at various elevations and alternating with beds of sand. The upper clay beds, covered by a considerable depth of white sand which is constantly found near the surface, are of a fine pipe clay, which at 'Big Durley' chine has at various times been worked out, and very considerable quantities of it sent to the potteries in Staffordshire. The beds of this clay, running under Poole harbour, and which are extensively worked on the Isle of Purbeck side, provide the purest and best material for the finest porcelain manufactured in this country. The clay beds which occur lower down in the cliffs, are of a dark bituminous character, and occasionally of considerable thickness. These beds, more especially on the east of Bournemouth, are full of vegetable remains. About half a mile in this direction the cliffs are composed of alternations of the white, yellow, and grey sands, overlaying strata of clay, divided by thin layers of vegetable matter. In a bed of white sand near the middle of the cliff, are impressions of ferns, and a layer of sandy clay is full of small leaves. Somewhat further on are strata of sand and sandy clay, abounding with beautiful vegetable remains. The plants are frequently so well preserved that the epidermis peels off when the specimen is exposed. They belong to genera of a warmer climate than that which now prevails in Great Britain.

The whole line of coast is much indented with those characteristic chines that constitute a feature of the district. These ravines are in several instances of great depth, with vertical sides, and are constantly varying in their aspect. One of them near Bourne has been deepened twenty feet within a few years. The formation of these excavations is chiefly owing to the existence of a spring at the head of each, the waters of which gradually wash away the sand, &c., producing these narrow ravines, which are sometimes from one hundred to one hundred and fifty feet deep. The largest and most remarkable are Boscomb chine and another to the eastward of Bournemouth; and Durley chines and Alum chine to the westward. The aspect of this coast is also constantly undergoing alteration by the extensive landslips that take place after severe frosts.

The valley of the Bourne is remarkable for the existence of some peat beds containing great numbers of trees deeply embedded. In regard to these is subjoined the following abstract of a paper read some time since, at a meeting of the Geological Society, —" On the peat bogs and sub-marine forests of Bournemouth, Hampshire, and in the neighbourhood of Poole, Dorsetshire," by the Rev. W. B. Clarke, F. G. S.

"The entrance of Bournemouth valley is one of the many chines which intersect the tertiary strata between Poole harbour and Christchurch head, and the valley extends from the sea three and a half miles in a N.W. direction. About half way a fork diverges to the west, and this branch, with the lower portion of the main valley, is called Bourne-bottom, and the eastern branch of the fork, Knighton-bottom. In each valley is a small current, and their united waters form the brook of Bournemouth. At the head of Knighton-bottom is a peat bog, which contains trunks of oak, alder, birch, and beech trees, also hazel sticks and nuts, and fragments of bark. The trunks of the trees lie in the direction of the valley, but the stools are firmly fixed upright in the peat. The wood, when extracted, is soft, but it becomes firm on exposure to the weather, and it is used for purposes of husbandry. The bark, especially that of the beech, retains its character unaltered. The surrounding district is now sterile, and no oaks of equal size exist within many miles of Knighton-bottom, the neighbouring plantations being of very recent origin. Traces of fire and of the axe are said to have been noticed in the bog wood. Ten feet of peat have been excavated, but the depth of the deposit is not known. The peasantry have a tradition that the forest was burned down during the reign of Stephen, though the writer of the paper conceives that its destruction was effected during the occupation of England by the Romans. At the head of Bourne-bottom there is also a peat bog, but it encloses only fir trees. There is a sub-marine peat bog and forest off the entrance to Bourne, of which an account was first given by Mr. Lyell, in his Principles of Geology, containing fir, beech, and alder trees." At low water spring tides, after a gale, portions of trees may frequently here be seen.

A geologist residing at Bournemouth, would find himself midway between the extraordinary and highly interesting geological peculiarities observable in the Isle of Wight, and the so called Isle of Purbeck, with speedy and easy access to either point.

Botany.—The immediate neighbourhood of Bournemouth does not offer a very rich field for the researches of the botanist. It is not, however, destitute of interesting features in this respect; and the dark hills which give the prevailing character to the district, present a variety of heaths; and the agrostis cetacea, *Curt.*, the only grass that will flourish on these hills during the dry season, is so abundant as to constitute, with its rigid and shining panicles, a striking feature. Descending, however, from the high ground, the valley, and particularly the peat beds, offer much pleasing employment to the botanical student. In regard to these tracts, we quote the following observations of Dr. Salter, of Ryde, Isle of Wight, in his valuable paper illustrative of the Botany of the neighbourhood, given as an appendix to Sydenham's History of Poole.

" In these situations the rhyncospora alba, *Vahl.*, and rhyncospora fusca, *Lin.*, abound, with many other of the cyperaceæ, of which the most general is schœnus nigricans, *Lin.* The heaths blossom freely in these districts, particularly the erica tetralix, *Lin.*, and the botany of them in general is very similar to that of the more northern regions. I do not mean to infer that the rarer northern plants are found with us, but that the bulk of vegetation in these situations is much the same as in similar soil in Cumberland and Scotland; as for example, the two ericæ and the calluna grow in profusion, with the melica cœrulea, *Lin.*, and myrica gale, *Lin.*, of which there are hundreds of acres in the south-east of Dorsetshire.

" Many parts of the more superficial bogs are adorned with the splendid flowers of gentiana pneumonanthe, *Lin.*, as well as with the three droseræ and anagallis tenalla, *Lin.*, all of which, together with pinguicula lusitanica, *Lin,*, exacum filiforme, *Sm.* and both varieties of scirpus Savii, *Spreng.*, may be esteemed common plants in our bogs."

Conchology.—The conchologist may derive much amusement from a ramble on the beach, where, under certain conditions of the tide, many specimens of the English marine shells may be found.   Amongst those which have been found on this beach, we may cite the following :—

Multivalves.	*Bivalves.*
Chiton fascicularis	Solen siliqua
———— marginatus	—— ensis
———— cinereus	—— legumen
———— albus	—— fragilis
Balanus intertextus	—— vespertinus
Pholas dactylus	Tellina ferroensis
———— candida	———— depressa
	———— fabula
Bivalves	———— tenuis
	———— punicea
Mya arenaria	———— reticulata
——— pretenuis	

Bivalves.

Tellina crassa
———— lactea
———— rotundata
———— carnaria
———— bimaculata
Cardium exiguum
———— echinatum
———— ciliare
———— levigatum
———— edule
Mactra stultorum
———— solida
———— subtruncata
———— Listeri
———— Boysii
———— lutraria
———— hians
Donax trunculus
Venus verrucosa
———— Gallina
———— Islandica
———— ovata
———— tigerina
———— exoleta
———— decussata
———— pullastra
———— virginea
———— aurea
Arca lactea
———— pilosa
———— nucleus
Ostrea opercularis
———— Jacobæa
———— varia
———— sinuosa
———— edulis
———— lineata

Bivalves.

Anomia ephippium
———— cepa
Mytilus edulis
———— discors
———— barbatus
Pinna pectinata

Univalves.

Nautilus crispus
———— Beccarii
Cypræa pediculus
———— arctica
Bulla haliotoidea
———— hydatis
———— obtusa
Buccinum lineatum
———— undatum
———— ambiguum
———— macula
Strombus pes pelecani
———— costatus
Murex erinaceus
———— antiquus
———— corneus
———— reticulatus
Trochus magnus
———— lineatus
———— umbilicatus
———— crassus
———— papillosus
———— zizyphinus
Turbo littoreus
———— tenebrosus
———— labiosus
———— clathrus
———— parvus
———— striatulus

Univalves.	Univalves..
Turbo terebra	Serpula spirorbis
—— truncatus	—— vermicularis
Nerita glaucina	—— seminulum
Dentallum entalis	Sabella granulata
Serpula spirillum	—— lumbricalis
—— triquetra	

THE NEIGHBOURHOOD.

This little book would be incomplete as a Guide, were not attention directed to the various objects of interest in the vicinity, within reach of an easy drive.

PARKSTONE,—POOLE,—LONGFLEET.

We proceed first to the westward, in which direction, after passing over about three miles of plantations, the tourist is brought to the crest of Parkstone hill, from many points of which a splendid view is spread before him, bounded by the distant Purbeck hills, and comprising the great basin of Poole harbour, with its diversified shores. This magnificent arm of the sea, more especially when the tide is in, presents much scenic beauty. The water, nearly surrounding the town, spreading a surface of indistinct extent, broken by islands and projecting headlands;—the shores, of a diversified character, here rising abruptly, there retiring in a low flat, and in many parts richly wooded;—the bustling port in the fore-ground, with its gallant array of masts and flags;—the back-ground, formed by the bold and well defined outline of the lofty Purbeck hills, giving relief to the sombre ruins of Corfe castle, mellowed by distance;—the island and castle of Branksea, forming a pleasing termination to one side of the view, whilst the other is bounded by the undulations of the distant heathy hills; combine to produce scenery of a very distinctive and agreeable kind. And as the communication between the harbour and the sea is hidden by the overlapping of Branksea island and the opposite sand banks, the appearance is that of a large inland lake. The delightful and much wooded village of *Parkstone* lies in the immediate fore-ground, the recently erected church, from its picturesque situation, constituting a prominent and pleasing object; and on descending the hill, the eye is pleased with the frequency of commodious houses tastefully erected in a cottage style, with lawns and shrubberies attached. The village is an extensive suburb of the adjacent town of Poole, and from its scenic beauties, convenient distance from the town, and its proximity to the sea, it has, within the last few years been much frequented, so that its population is rapidly increasing. It was in this hamlet that the manufacture of alum was first commenced in England; Lord Mountjoy, who at that time possessed the manor, having established works here so early as 1564, for that purpose. These works were discontinued after some years, but an unsuccessful attempt to revive them was made by the Earl of Huntingdon, at the commencement of the seventeenth century. After this establishment went to decay salterns were constructed here; but these, also, are now in ruins, not having been worked for many years. Parkstone was without a church until within the last few years; and for all ecclesiastical purposes, the inhabitants had to resort to the church of Canford, five miles distant. The present church is a neat structure, erected in 1833. It was consecrated by the bishop of Bristol, on the 20th of September in that year. An ecclesiastical district has since been set apart for it, comprising the whole of the hamlet of Parkstone. A Sunday school has been established in connection with the church, and is well encouraged.

There is also a very neat Independent chapel, which is attended by a numerous congregation, and has Sunday schools in connection with it.

From Parkstone, we proceed to enter the contiguous sea port town of *Poole.* This is a town of considerable antiquity, though it presents few buildings or other prominent objects of archæological interest. It is neatly built, and remarkably clean, standing on a peninsula which juts into the harbour, and is joined to the mainland by a narrow and short isthmus. It occupies a considerable tract of ground, being nearly one mile long and three quarters of a mile broad. The principal streets run parallel, from N.E. to S.W., and the minor streets and intersecting lanes are very numerous. The houses, which are generally commodious and respectable, have been built with more regard to convenience and comfort, than to regularity and exterior splendour. The town

is the most considerable in the county of Dorset;
and since the middle of the sixteenth century, when
the influx of inhabitants and several grants from
favouring monarchs combined to encourage its trade
and general prosperity, it has acquired much maritime
importance. The principal foreign trade is with the
colonies of Newfoundland and British North America;
but mercantile transactions with other foreign parts
are now engaged in, and since the free importation of
foreign corn has been permitted, great quantities of
foreign wheat and other grain have been imported, and
as nearly all is brought in foreign bottoms, many
Dutch and French vessels are frequently to be seen
alongside the extensive quay. Prussian and Swedish
vessels also frequently discharge cargoes of timber
here. There is in addition an extensive coasting trade,
Poole being the port of supply to a considerable
tract of inland country.

The principal structures of antiquarian interest in
the town, are the Town Cellars on the quay, probably
erected in the fourteenth century as a place of
deposit for the customs and tallages then taken by
the seignorial lord;—a small remaining portion, in
St. Clement's lane, of the wall with which the town
was fortified in the reigns of Henry VI. and Richard
III;—and a few houses in the lower part of the
town, which indicate some antiquity.

The *Parish Church of Saint James*, Poole, was
erected in 1820, on the site of an antient church then
demolished. It is a large and commodious edifice,

consisting of a nave and two aisles, with a small
chancel, but possessing, externally, little architectural
beauty. At the west end is a tower in which are
eight bells. The appearance of the interior of
the church, on entering it by the west door, is
very pleasing, and derives much effect from the
large and lofty east window of painted glass, representing Faith, personified in a female figure kneeling
on the cross, with the open bible and the cup of the
new testament before her, gazing upwards, whence
a flood of light is poured on her. The window is
divided by two mullions, and this painting occupies
the middle compartment. The ceiling, which is
supported by lofty but inelegant columns, is neatly
groined. A spacious gallery runs round the church,
excepting at the east end. All the monuments now in
the church are mural, several of them possessing
much elegance.

The *Church of Saint Paul* stands towards the
upper end of the High-street. This church was
erected a few years since, and was consecrated in
1833, to meet the religious wants of the increasing
population of the town, the church of St. James, even
in its new and enlarged state, being inadequate to the
demand for church accommodation. It is a small
and neat structure, in a Greco-Roman style, and contains about seven hundred sittings, of which two
hundred are free. The east front is surmounted by
a cupola.

The *Meeting-houses* of the various dissenting congregations are those of the Independents, in Skinner-street; the Unitarians, in Hill-street; the Baptists, in Hill-street; the Wesleyan Methodists, in Chapel-lane; the Friends, in Lagland-street; and the Primitive Methodist, in North-street; there is also a very neat Popish chapel, erected at West-butts.

The principal other public buildings, are the *Guildhall*, which stands in the market-place, and is a spacious and convenient structure, comprising a council chamber, a large hall of justice, retiring rooms for the jury, &c., having on the ground story a series of open arcades, occupied on market days by the butchers;—the *Public Library*, situated at the lower extremity of the High-street, near the quay, having been founded in 1830. The room containing the library, is lofty, sufficiently large, and well adapted to the purpose. The institution is supported by donations and annual subscriptions; strangers are admitted to the reading room on the introduction of a member;—the *Town House*, a building which has been erected for the convenience of merchants and others, as a news room and place of general resort. It is supplied with the leading London daily journals, provincial newspapers, and other periodical publications. To this institution, also, access is easy to the stranger, through the introduction of a member;—the *Custom House*, a commodious and well-arranged building, centrally and con- veniently situated on the quay;—the *Gaol*, standing in King-street;—the *National School*, a large building, well adapted to the purpose, erected in 1835, at Perry-garden, and in which about 150 boys and 100 girls are generally under education. The *British School* is also a commodious building, patronised principally by the independent dissenters, and in which an equal number of children to those in the national schools, receive instruction.

In 1849 was established a " Literary Scientific and Mechanics Institution," which has hitherto been very well supported. There is, in connection with it, an extensive and well selected library, a museum, to which the friends of the Institution solicit further contributions, and a reading and news room, which is very liberally supplied with newspapers and magazines. The house in which the association is at present located is of an unpretending appearance, situated at the lower part of the high-street, though it is hoped that not many years will elapse before a building worthy the town is erected for the purpose. In connection with this society, lectures are given almost weekly during six months in the year, the Town Hall being used for the lecture room.

The markets of Poole are spacious and convenient, and very well supplied, in regard both to the quality and quantity of the meat, vegetables, fruit, &c., brought for sale; and the prices in general are considerably lower than those of most other markets. The market days are Monday and Thursday. The fish market is holden in a modern edifice, built for the purpose, on the quay; and the harbour and adjoining coast are tolerably productive of fish. Those principally caught for the table are mackerel, herring, whiting, cod, turbot, brill, soles, plaice, skate, gray mullett, red mullett, barce, eels, lobsters, crabs, oysters, cockles, muscles, and perriwinkles.

Wagons, for the conveyance of goods, to and from any part of the country, regularly arrive in and depart from the town. Packets, likewise, constantly ply between Poole and London, Portsmouth, Southampton, Swanage, Wareham, and other ports. There is a packet, also, that sails to and returns from the islands of Guernsey and Jersey, and it is expected that there will very soon be regular steam communication to the Channel Islands, the passage between them and Poole, being the shortest and most convenient of any.

The London and general mail arrives here about, 3 A.M,, letters being delivered at 7, and leaves at 10 P,M., the letter box closing twenty-five minutes before that hour; there is also a day mail leaving for the eastward at half-past 10 A.M., and for the westward at 3 P.M.

The estuary of the sea, on which the town of Poole stands, is very extensive, and highly picturesque. Stretching many miles inland, it presents to the observer very pleasing varieties of scenery, whilst it offers to the mariner a haven almost always accessible. The entrance to the harbour is very narrow, and lies between two long ranges of sand banks, one projecting from the north-east part of the Isle of Purbeck, called South-haven point, the other extending from the mainland of Dorsetshire, and termed North-haven point, The distance between those is about a furlong. Directly opposite to this entrance is the island of Branksea with its striking castellated mansion. This island divides the stream, of which the largest and navigable branch flows to the northward and leads to Poole. The harbour extends from hence, amidst winding shores and picturesque headlands, up to the marshes adjoining Wareham, washing the borders of many a little island, and sweeping within a short distance of the sombre ruins of Corfe Castle.

Poole, with the adjoining parishes and tythings, has been formed into a Poor Law Union, the workhouse of which is situate in the adjacent hamlet of Longfleet.

The borough of Poole constitutes a county of itself. It was formerly co-extensive with the parish of Saint James, but by the recent Parliamentary and Municipal Reform Acts, the boundaries were extended so as to include the adjoining hamlets of Hamworthy, Parkstone, and Longfleet. The borough returns two members to Parliament.

Poole became a thoroughfare by the erection of a bridge across the channel of the harbour which divides Hamworthy from the town. The middle arch of this bridge is constructed on the swivel principle, so as to afford easy passage to vessels. By its erection and the contemporaneous alteration of some of the roads in the neighbourhood, the distance by Turn-pike road between Poole and Blandford, Wareham, and other towns to the west, was lessened by about two miles.

Passing over this bridge we reach the pleasant village of *Hamworthy*, seated in a delightful combination of rural and marine scenery. Immediately contiguous to the bridge is the Poole Station of the South Western Railway. The church of Hamworthy about a mile distant from this point, the drive to which is through a prettily wooded lane, is a neat structure, erected in 1826.

Should the tourist be disposed to extend the drive round the bay dividing Hamworthy from Poole, he will be amply repaid by the very pleasing scenery, presented by the picturesque association of wood and water. At the head of this bay, about two and a half miles from Poole, is placed Upton House, the seat of Sir Edward Doughty, Bart., standing on a gentle eminence, well environed with wood, and commanding extensive and most agreeable prospects. Pursuing this route, after passing over Creekmoor bridge, up to which the tidal waters of the bay regularly flow, we reach the immediate neighbourhood of Poole through the hamlet of

Longfleet, which also has a district church. It was opened for divine service on September 25th, 1833. The visitor from Bournemouth has no occasion to re-enter the town of Poole, as a road through the north-east part of this hamlet will conduct him into the village of Parkstone, before alluded to.

LITTLEDOWN,—ENSBURY,—CANFORD. &c.

Leaving Bournemouth in a northerly direction and crossing the adjacent heath, we arrive, about two miles distant, at *Littledown House ;* a house commandingly placed on a declivity, the seat of Mrs. Clapcott. Passing this and crossing the main road from Christchurch to Wimborne, we reach the pleasant and secluded villages of *Holdenhurst* and *Throop.* At the former of these places a very neat and chastely designed church has been recently erected in the room of the antient structure, which was both inconvenient and of limited accommodation. The river Stour, which irrigates this fertile valley, passes through this parish on its way to the sea, which it meets below Christchurch. On the opposite bank of the river is the majestic mansion of *Heron Court,* the seat of the Earl of Malmesbury, placed in an extensive park, possessing much delightful scenery, and surrounded by plantations extending over about two thousand acres. The following notice of this seat is from a small and very pleasing volume recently published, being a "Historical and descriptive account

of the Town and Borough of Christchurch," &c. ;—
" This noble mansion was for a long period in the
possession of the family of the late Edward Hooper,
Esq., the representative, in several successive parlia-
ments, of the borough of Christchurch; it is now the
property and residence of the Earl of Malmesbury,
to whose late grandfather, the near relative of Mr.
Hooper, it was bequeathed. It has, subsequently,
been considerably enlarged and improved, and is an
elegant specimen of the modern Gothic, the whole of
the offices being in the same beautiful style of architecture. The entrance is by a spacious hall, which
leads to the different suites of apartments, Many of
the rooms contain some fine paintings, including
several original portraits of the royal family. The
magnificent library comprises the invaluable collection
of his lordship's ancestor, James Harris, esq., the
erudite author of ' Hermes' and other philological
works, to which great additions have since been made
in modern literature. In the gardens are a variety
of indigenous and exotic shrubs, tastefully arranged."

Returning to the main road, we proceed onwards
to the pleasantly situated and picturesque villages of
Ensbury and *Kinson*, leaving which and crossing the
turnpike road from Poole to Longham, we reach the
charming village of *Canford*, with the splendid edifice
of Canford House, the seat of Sir Josiah John Guest,
Bart., M.P., in which are now located many beautiful
specimens of Assyrian antiquities discovered at Mosul
and Nimroud, by that enterprising explorer, Mr.

Layard, an intimate friend of the owner of the demesne. This manorial mansion is an elegant and commodious house in the style of the domestic architecture of the Tudor age, built from a design of Edward Blore, esq., about 1825, but very considerably enlarged by the present proprietor since it came into his possession by purchase, in 1847, from the Right Honorable Lord de Mauley. It is delightfully situated on the southern bank of the Stour, standing on the spot formerly occupied by the antient mansion of the lords of the manor. The venerable structure pulled down that the present edifice might be reared, though evidently erected at various periods, bore testimony, in every part, to its claims to considerable antiquity, and for many years before its demolition was one of the rarest specimens of our early mansion houses. A portion of it was, not improbably coeval with William Longespee, Earl of Salisbury, (son of Henry II., by that celebrated beauty, the " fair Rosamond"), who held the manor, and occasionally resided here. King John, also, the half-brother of Longespee, was a frequent visitor at Canford. Indeed there are few places in the country invested with more interesting historical associations. Striking and varied have been the scenes which the antique walls of the " gray old house" witnessed during the lapse of nearly seven centuries. The virtues and the sorrows of the gentle Ela, of Salisbury; the honours of the heroic Longespee; the romantic elopement of Maud de Clifford; the unfortunate life of Alice de Lacy; the glories of the Montacutes; the renown of

John, the great Duke of Somerset; the learning and devotion of Margaret of Richmond; and the piety of Gertrude of Exeter, sufficed to invest with no common interest the mansion successively occupied by these personages. The only portion of the antient house now remaining is the old kitchen, which stands apart from the house, and for which the neighbours, but without any authority, have traditionally preserved the appellation of John of Gaunt's kitchen. This spacious and characteristic building, with its gigantic fire-places, speaks powerfully to the imagination of the manners and hospitalities of former days,—of the times when the proud baron sat surrounded by a gallant company, and feasted in his halls a numerous retinue of armed servitors. Long may it stand to connect the present day with the romantic incidents associated with the more remote history of the mansion.

About a mile from Canford is the town of *Wimborne*, with its venerable minster, which is well worth a visit. This antient structure has recently been restored at a great expence, and now offers to the gratified eye of the visitor a rare and noble specimen of our early ecclesiastical architecture. There is in the town a liberally endowed and well-conducted Free Grammar School, the head master of which is the Rev. W. Fletcher, D.D.

E

BOSCOMB,—STOURFIELD,—IFORD,—CHRISTCHURGH.

About two miles from Bournemouth, to the eastward, on the road to Christchurch, is *Boscomb Lodge*, a comfortable country seat, late in the occupation of Major Stephenson.   A bye-road, about a furlong in extent, will here conduct the visitor to Boscomb chine, but this may be better visited from the beach.   A short distance further, situated on a commanding eminence a few hundred yards from the beach, is *Stourfield House* the seat of Captain Popham, R.N., by whom it has been recently purchased from the executors of the late Sir G. W. Tapps Gervis, Bart. From many points in the vicinity of this establishment the views are romantic, extensive, beautiful, and varied.   The Countess of Strathmore passed here in retirement, the latter years of her eventful life, having died in 1800, in this house, whence her remains were removed to Westminster Abbey for interment.   Proceeding onward, we soon reach the village of *Iford*, a place of great antiquity, and historically distinguished as the theatre of some skirmishes in 901, between the forces of Edward the elder and those of Ethelwald, which latter, rising against Edward, seized upon Christchurch and Wimborne; and Edward, taking possession of Badbury Rings, drove his enemies from Wimborne, and defeated them in a conflict at this place, then known as Yattingford.   Here is the residence of W. D. Farr, Esq., a neat modern erection, presented to view through a vista formed by a double row of stately elms. Crossing the Stour by a long, narrow, and antient bridge, composed of fourteen arches, we pass *Jumper s*, a quiet country residence, situated in an extremely pleasant locality, and a little further on reach an extensive range of barracks, erected about fifty years since, containing stables and gun sheds for the accommodation of horse artillery, a troop of which was generally stationed here during the last war; since that time the barracks have been occasionally occupied by detachments of dragoons from the head quarters at Dorchester.

About half a mile further we enter the antient town of *Christchurch*, situated near the confluence of the rivers Stour and Avon, which, flowing on either side of it, unite their streams a short distance below, and pour their united waters into the sea. It is a clean and neat town, formed of three principal streets, which meet in the market place, where is placed the town-hall, built on open arcades in which the market is held. In the centre of the principal front of this building is a pediment and pierced entablature, supported upon Doric pilasters; and in the centre of the building is a small cupola and clock-turret.

Christchurch is as antient as the Saxon era, and was occupied by Ethelwald during his revolt against his kinsman, Edward the elder; it contains several interesting relics of its former importance.

The Castle.—Near the church, and somewhat to the north of it and the priory, are the remains of the Castle, erected by Richard de Redvers, or Ripariis, Earl of Devon, in the time of Henry I., that monarch having presented the manor to the Earl. These ruins comprise that part of the range containing the state apartments, and form a very picturesque object, being seated immediately on the west bank of the Avon ; whilst the dilapidated walls covered with ivy, the Anglo-Norman arches and pillars, and decorations, not only serve to gratify the eye of those who seek merely scenic beauty, but to those who love to linger amidst the relics of antient art, and to speculate on the associations with which the monuments of the antique time are invested, they recal many a scene of noisy festivity—many an instance of the chastening influence of chivalric feeling—many a proud display of the power and wealth of the feudal lord, within the walls which now present so pleasingly sad a contrast to these things, in their state of silence, desertion, and ruin. And the ruder and more massive walls of the ruined keep, standing, as it were, aloof in the solitude of their desolation, also tell their tale of war, of sorrow, and of death.

The Priory.—The old priory, which gives its present name to the town, was of Saxon foundation, having been founded prior to the conquest for a dean and twenty-four secular canons. Some portions of the walls that enclosed the conventual buildings are still remaining; the antient lodge, a strongly built stone edifice, is now occupied as a dwelling house, and the site of the refectory may be traced by the remnants of its walls These remains, however, are not part of the original structure, but of the buildings raised by Ralph Flambard, Bishop of Durham, and formerly dean of the priory, which he re-built in the reign of William II. On the site of the priory a large mansion was built some years since, by Gustavus Brander, Esq., which became the residence, in 1807, of Louis Philippe, Duke of Orleans, the late King of the French.

The Church.—The most prominent object of interest to the antiquary and the lover of art, is the antient priory church. This edifice, which, equally in its extent and arrangement as in its principal details, exhibits all the magnificence of a cathedral, stands on a pleasant spot, (the ground being slightly elevated,) near the south-western extremity of the town. From the leads, both of the tower and roof, it commands a most beautiful prospect, seaward, over the bay, Hengistbury Head, the English Channel, and the western parts of the Isle of Wight; and on the land side, of the rich meadows surrounding the town, watered by the sinuous streams of the Avon and the Stour, of St. Catherine's hill, and of a widely spread reach of country, extending over a great part of the New Forest. In its general design, this church comprehends a nave and two aisles; a transept with chapels projecting eastward; a choir and its aisles; a lady chapel ; a western tower, and a capacious north porch. So much variety and grandeur, intelligence and taste, are displayed in its architecture, that we cannot but regret the deficiency of records which prevents our ascertaining by whom, and at what exact periods, the different divisions of the noble fabric were respectively erected. With the exception, indeed, of the Norman part,—the undoubted work of Bishop Flambard, and his early successors in this deanery,— we are unacquainted with any historical document whatsoever that will enable us indubitably to assign any other portion of the church to any known individual ; and we can scarcely affix a date to any part beyond the transept, except by inferences drawn from the style and execution of other similar buildings, of which the age is unquestionable.

For a very long period this church, notwithstanding the highly interesting character of its architecture, underwent great dilapidation, and suffered from extreme neglect ; scarcely any thing being done to it except obliterating its sculpture by thick coatings of whitewash, and blocking up windows instead of repairing them, in compliance with the too frequent dictates of parochial economy. Since the commencement, however, of the present century, and more especially during the respective curacies of the late Rev. William Bingley, A.M., (the well known naturalist and antiquary), his very estimable successor, the Rev. Richard Waldy, A.M., and the present vicar, the Rev. W. F. Burrows, A.M., and ~ided by their own praiseworthy exertions, such numerous repairs and alterations have been effected here, that the interior has assumed an entirely new aspect, and the exterior has been much improved.

We proceed to take a rapid survey of the more striking exterior features, and shall then conduct the visitor to the interior of this beautiful fabric. There are two entrances to the church, namely from the western tower, and from the north porch. The tower is of a square form, of a massive character, good proportions, and well built. The entrance portal is formed by a pointed arch, having spandrils at the sides. The present great pointed arched window, which was rebuilt a few years ago, is fifteen feet in width, and thirty-four feet in height. Within an embellished niche over the window is a full sized effigy of our Saviour. The belfry contains eight bells. Passing round the north-west angle of the tower, we reach the principal entrance to the church, the north porch, which in respect to size and massiveness of construction, is probably unequalled by any other in this country. Its projection is upwards of forty feet, and in height it almost extends to the parapet of the main building. The most interesting feature of this porch is the wide-spreading and deeply-recessed pointed arch, which forms the direct entrance to the church through two enclosed cinque-foil headed doorways. The exterior of the north aisle presents nothing requiring remark; but the north division of the transept offers a very curious and probably unique example of Norman architectural decoration, for the scientific details of which, however, we must be content with refering the reader to Mr. Brayley's elaborate account given in " Ferrey's Antiquities of Christchurch;" from which indeed this brief sketch is mainly abridged. All the parts eastward of the transept are designed in the pointed style, and preserve a general similarity of form and character. Some handsome tracery, though not florid, is displayed in the choir windows. The windows of the lady chapel are well proportioned and of elegant design. Passing under the great east window, we arrive at the southern side of the church. In the southern division of the transept, and thence westward to nearly the extremity of the fabric, the Norman architecture again predominates, and the southern exterior of the nave preserves much of its original character. The antient cloisters are reported to have been connected with this side of the church.

On entering the church from the west door-way an excellent view is obtained of the nave, which furnishes a splendid example of the later and more decorated style of Norman architecture; in which respect there is, probably, no building in the kingdom that can vie with it. Here, amidst the noble semicircular arches and complicated piers, the bold buildings and curiously sculptured capitols, the compartments of the triforium, the peculiarities of the elevated clerestory, and the innovated dissimilarities between the north and south aisles, the architectural student and the admirer of art may indulge in contemplations and associations as pleasing as instructive. Through the transept, which merits much attention, we pass to the choir under a stone screen, which, prior to the reformation, supported the rood-loft. It was originally very beautiful, but had been most disgracefully mutilated in comparatively modern times, indeed so much so, that the lovers of church architecture of the neighbourhood made frequent attempts for its restoration, but were unsuccessful in their good intentions until February, 1848, when, at a vestry meeting specially convened, a liberal subscription having before been made for the purpose, it was resolved that the screen should be restored. It was then in so dilapidated a state that but little more than sufficient of its beauties remained to give an idea of its original appearance. The work of restoration was undertaken by Mr. Rowe, sculptor of Exeter, by whom it was most faithfully performed; and the rood screen is once again a striking ornament of this beautiful church. Independently of the light and elegant character of its architecture, the choir furnishes various objects of much interest; the western part, which is wainscoted with oak, is chiefly occupied by the antient stalls and sub-seats of the priory of the establishment. On the back, arms, and jambs of the stalls, as well as on the *misereries*, or under seats, there is a profusion of carving in alto or bas-relief, including many representations of a grotesque and satirical character, which are supposed to refer to the selfish arts of the mendicant friars, who began to establish themselves in England in the thirteenth century. The altar-piece, or screen, is designed with great elegance, and when perfect, must have been extremely rich as a specimen of sculptured architecture. The subject is the genealogy of Christ, with the adoration of the Magi. To the north of the altar is the beautiful monumental chapel of the celebrated Margaret, Countess of Salisbury. The general design of this structure is in the Tudor style, and the interior, especially, is of the richest architectural composition, the roof being formed of beautiful fan-like tracery, springing from sculptured corbels, and ornamented by rich bosses. Both fronts of this elegant specimen of scientific art are highly ornamented. The choir aisles deserve much attention from their architectural features, and from the chapels and monuments which they contain. The eastern extremity of the church is terminated by the lady chapel, evidently erected at nearly the same period as the choir. Over the altar in this chapel are the dilapidated remains of a very beautiful stone screen of rich tabernacle work.

The church contains several interesting chapels and remarkable monuments; of the former, besides that of the Countess of Salisbury, already noticed, are two small chantry chapels or oratories in the east end of the north aisle; another on the south side of the north choir aisle; an antient chapel in the south choir aisle; the chantry and sepulchral chapel of Robert

Harys, on the north side of the same aisle; and occupying the western division of this aisle, is the chantry chapel of John Draper, the last prior of that name, who died in 1552. The more distinguished of the monuments are an altar tomb, on which lie the effigies of a knight and his lady, said traditionally to have been raised to the memory of Sir John Chideoke and his lady, of Chideoke, Dorset; and an eminently beautiful monumental group, by Flaxman, sculptured to the memory of Viscountess Fitzharris, the mother of the present earl of Malmesbury, representing that estimable lady instructing her children from the Holy Scriptures in their religious and moral duties. There are also several monumental inscriptions of priors of the antient priory, and a number of mural monuments.

From researches made by Mr. Brander, who purchased the priory estate some years since, there seems reason to conclude that the site of the priory had been occupied by a pagan temple, which was afterwards converted to Christian uses.

The town of Christchurch contains little more of public interest. There are several meeting-houses, for the use of dissenting congregations.

In the neighbourhood of Christchurch are several pleasant villages.

THE BEACH.—HENGISTBURY HEAD,—THE CHINES,— BRANKSEA.

We have now but to call the attention of the visitor to the principal objects observable in a stroll on the *Beach*. This delightful shore, extending from Hengistbury head to the entrance of Poole harbour, offers at all times a promenade surrounded by objects of great interest. The appearance of the sea, varying in its character with every change of the wind or weather, constitutes of itself a scene of never-ending charm; whilst the distant vessels passing respectively up or down the channel, freighted not more with merchandize than with human hopes and fears; the smaller craft skirting closer to the coast, and the light fishing boats dancing from wave to wave, present abundant food for speculative contemplation. During the mackerel and herring seasons animated and picturesque scenes are witnessed along this beach, where the neighbouring fishermen assemble for the capture of the enormous shoals which annually visit this coast, the drawing of the seines, especially on moonlight evenings, producing a remarkable effect which can hardly be conceived by those who have not witnessed it.

Hengistbury Head, the high promontory which terminates the bay to the eastward, is surmounted by a rude entrenched earthwork of considerable magnitude, and of great interest to the antiquary. It is of irregular form, affecting the natural conformation of the hill, and consists of two ramparts and ditches. It is generally believed to be a work of Danish construction ; and tradition regards it as having been thrown up by Hengist, on his landing here after the death of Horsa, in Kent, and that the place thence derived the name it now bears. This opinion however, is open to much question. It is by no means certain that Hengist ever landed here, though such an event is not unlikely : but it is not in accordance with the policy of a maritime roving people like the Danes to construct a strong fortress in the immediate vicinity of their landing-place. If in their inland ravages they were compelled to retreat, they would naturally betake themselves, not to any laboured structure on land, but to their ships, which would at once remove them from the reach of their pursuers. And as this earthwork is entirely analogous to several similar entrenchments, the British origin of which is unquestionable, it may be more properly concluded that it was thrown up by the antient Celto-British tribes as a barrier to maritime encroachment; and that it might have been subsequently occupied temporarily by the forces of Hengist, if they landed, as surmised, in Christchurch harbour.

The many *Chines* which intersect the sand cliffs that bound the land on this part of the coast, and constitute so striking a geological feature in the formation, have frequently a picturesque wildness in their character, rendering them well worthy of a visit.

Following the beach to the entrance of Poole harbour, we arrive opposite the pleasing island of *Branksea*, with its castellated mansion. This island, though now fertile and wooded, was formerly a barren spot, with only one house upon it, and an old blockhouse fort, intended for the defence of the harbour. It is of an irregular oval form, in length about a mile and a half, and in breadth three quarters of a mile. After passing through the hands of various possessors, it became the property of the late Humphrey Sturt, Esq., who sold it to Sir Charles Chad, Bart., of Pinkney hall, near Fakenham, Norfolk, who about five years since, sold it to the Right Hon. Sir Augustus John Foster, of Stonehouse, in the county of Lough. The castle, which is on the south-east side of the island, forms a delightful marine residence; it possesses, however, little strength as a fortress of defence, though strong and effective batteries might easily be placed on the island, so as completely to command the entrance of the harbour.

Dr. Granville in his "Spas of England", published in 1841, says of Bournemouth—

" No situation that I have had occasion to examine along the whole southern coast, possesses so many capabilities of being made the very first invalid sea-watering place in England; and not only a watering place, but what is still more important, a winter residence for the most delicate constitutions, requiring a warm and sheltered locality at this season of the year. As such I hold it superior to either Bonchurch, St. Lawrence, or Ventnor, in the Isle of Wight. Though situated ten miles less to the south than the extreme point of that island, Bourne has the superior advantage of being rather more than as many miles to the westward, a circumstance that makes quite sufficient amends for the trifling difference in regard to its southern position. But Bourne has other claims to superiority over Ventnor, being in the centre of a beautiful curvilinear sweep of coast or bay, which, instead of being called Poole Bay, ought henceforth to be called Bourne Bay, the two extreme points or horns of which, equi-distant from Bourne, serve to protect the latter from the direct influence of many of the most objectionable winds. But above all is Bourne superior to the back of the Isle of Wight, from its entire exposure to the south, with a full protection from the easterly winds, to which Ventnor on the contrary is indirectly exposed. I hardly need touch upon its superiority as a bathing-place to any in the neighbourhood, or along these coasts. It is as an inland sheltered haven for the most tender invalids however that I would call your attention to the great capabilities of Bourne; for we look in vain elsewhere for that singular advantage which Bourne possesses, of presenting two banks of cliffs, clothed with verdure even at this inclement season, (the middle of January,) running from the sea inland, with a smiling vale watered by a rapid brook or bourne, dividing them just enough to allow of a most complete ventilation, with coolness in the summer months, and yet affording a most protected succession of ridges upon which to erect residences not only for convalescents, free from positive disease, but also for patients in the most delicate state of health as to lungs."

It is almost needless to say that Dr. Granville's opinion of Bournemouth is not singular, as since the above extract was penned by that gentleman, Bournemouth has gradually raised in public estimation, until it is now one of the most popular winter resorts for invalids requiring a highly sheltered locality.

DISTANCE FROM BOURNEMOUTH

To Poole,	5 miles	To Bath,	67 miles
Christchurch,	5 miles	Wareham,	13 miles
Lymington,	17 miles	Corfe Castle,	17 miles
Wimborne,	10 miles	Swanwich,	23 miles
Ringwood,	12 miles	Dorchester,	28 miles
Southampton,	28 miles	Weymouth,	34 miles
Salisbury,	30 miles	London,	104 miles

Visitors who desire the acquisition of further details relative to the neighbouring towns, &c., are referred to the following works:—

The History of the Town and County of Poole; collected and arranged from antient records and other authentic Documents, and deduced from the earliest period to the present time. By JOHN SYDENHAM. 8vo., plates, pp. 492.

Ductor Vindogladiensis: an Historical and Descriptive Guide to the Town of Wimborne Minster, Dorsetshire, with a particular account of the Collegiate Church of St. Cuthberge, the Chapel of St. Margaret, and other Charitable Endowments in the same parish. Small 8vo., plates, pp. 48.

Views of the Exterior and Interior of the Collegiate Church of St. Cuthberge, Wimborne Minster, Dorset. Drawn and engraved by N. WHITTOCK. With a concise History of the Church, and Description of the Plates. Illustrated also by Engravings on Wood. Large folio.

The Antiquities of the Priory of Christchurch, Hants, consisting of Plans, Sections, Elevations, Details, and Perspective : accompanied by Historical and Descriptive Accounts of the Priory Church ; together with some general particulars of the Castle and Borough.   By BENJAMIN FERRY, Architect. The Literary Part by EDWARD WEDLAKE BRAYLEY Esq., F.S.A., &c, 20 plates, quarto, pp, 116.

Historical and Descriptive Account of the Town and Borough of Christchurch ; comprehending a Guide to the Watering Places of Mudeford and Bournemouth ; with Brief Notices of the Seats of the Nobility and Gentry, the Picturesque Scenery, and Antiquities in the immediate neighbourhood. Small octavo, pp. 50.

www.ingramcontent.com/pod-product-compliance
Lightning Source LLC
Chambersburg PA
CBHW081525040426
42447CB00013B/3346

9 781535 814942